An Anti-Bullying Rap

Lorraine Simeon
and Rowan Clifford

VIKING

Published by the Penguin Group
Penguin Books Ltd, 27 Wrights Lane, London W8 5TZ, England
Penguin Books USA Inc., 375 Hudson Street, New York, New York 10014, USA
Penguin Books Australia Ltd, Ringwood, Victoria, Australia
Penguin Books Canada Ltd, 10 Alcorn Avenue, Toronto, Ontario, Canada M4V 3B2
Penguin Books (NZ) Ltd, 182–190 Wairau Road, Auckland 10, New Zealand

Penguin Books Ltd. Registered Offices: Harmondsworth, Middlesex, England

First published by Blackie 1994
Published by Viking 1995
10 9 8 7 6 5 4 3 2 1

Text copyright © Lorraine Simeon, 1994
Illustrations copyright © Rowan Clifford, 1994

The moral right of the author and illustrator have been asserted

All rights reserved. Without limiting the rights under copyright reserved above, no part of this publication may be reproduced, stored in or introduced into a retrieval system, or transmitted, in any form or by any means (electronic, mechanical, photocopying, recording or otherwise), without the prior written permission of both the copyright owner and the above publisher of this book.

Filmset in Crash Bang Wallop Light and Medium

Made and printed in Singapore

A CIP catalogue record for this book is available from the British Library

ISBN 0–670–85994–X Pbk

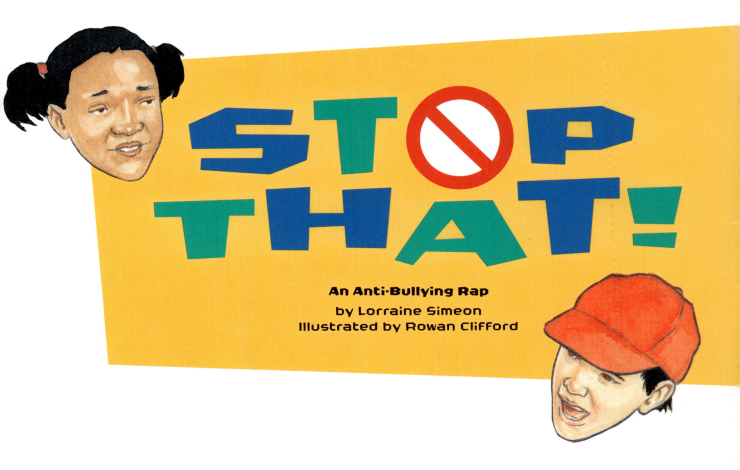

STOP THAT!

An Anti-Bullying Rap

by Lorraine Simeon
Illustrated by Rowan Clifford

VIKING

If you're old enough to go to school, you're old enough to know,
Your parents can't be with you, everywhere you go.

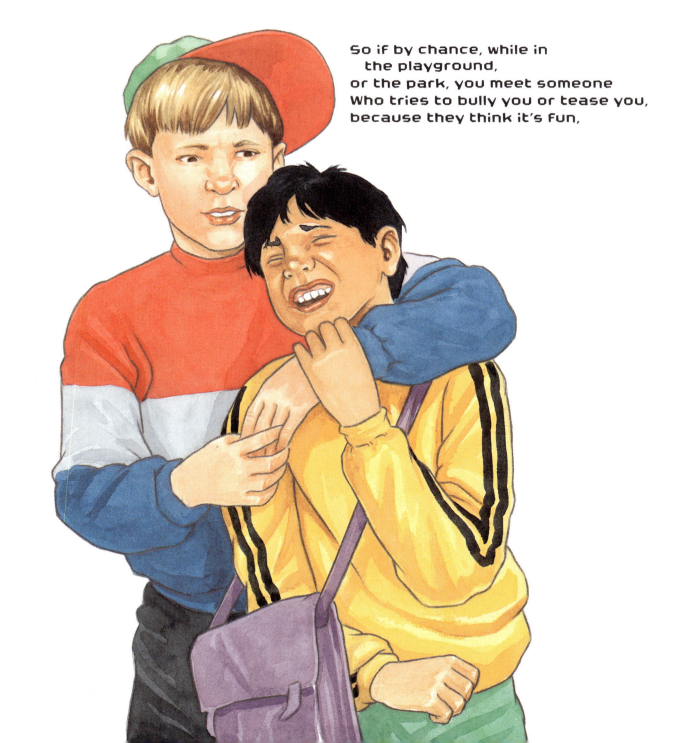

So if by chance, while in
  the playground,
or the park, you meet someone
Who tries to bully you or tease you,
because they think it's fun,

Don't let them see you're frightened,
if you can, just walk away,
Bullies are just cowards who
think bullying's okay.

They tell others not to be your friend,
as if they have the right,
Bullies pick on quiet kids,
bullies like to fight.

Bullies like to show you up so you feel weak and small,
They ask if they can play with you and then they take your ball.

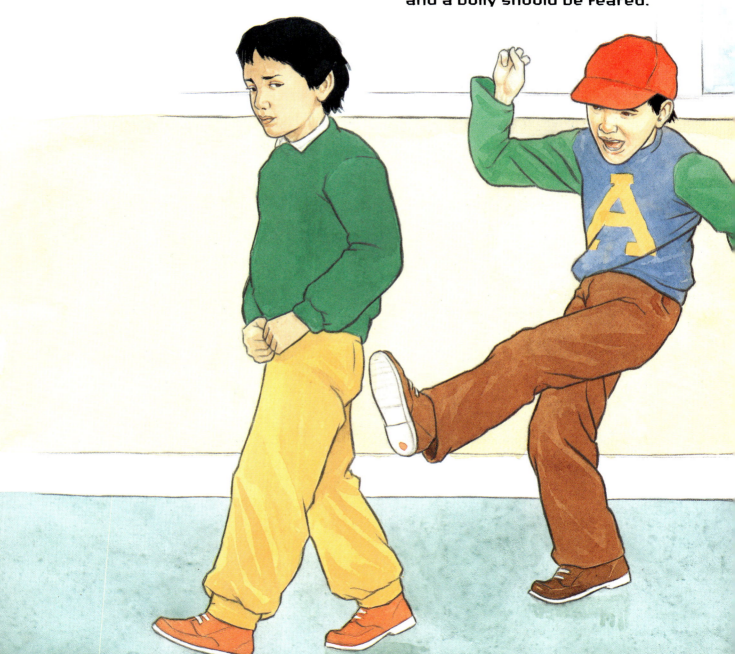

Bullies have a way of doing things,
that sometimes makes you scared,
As if bullying is power
and a bully should be feared.

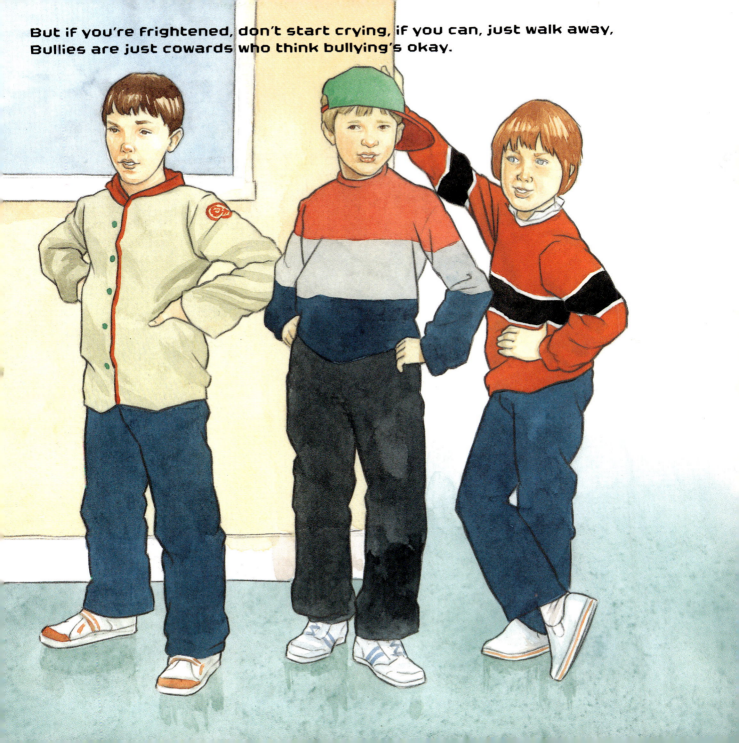

But if you're frightened, don't start crying, if you can, just walk away,
Bullies are just cowards who think bullying's okay.

Grown-ups, parents, teachers know that bullying is wrong,
It's important that you always let them know what's going on.

No one should be pushed around or made to feel so low,
That they're too frightened to tell anyone or let an adult know.

Taking on a bully is not an easy thing to do,
Especially if they're in a gang or twice as big as you.

Don't be afraid to call for help if you must stand your ground,
Bullies can't perform when you've got all your friends around.

If you think it's good to bully, then you'd better think again,
Even being in a bullies' gang can earn you a bad name.

Ganging up on someone is a spiteful thing to do,
Stop and think a moment, would you like it done to you?

Why not try out a new hobby,
find a sport you like to play,
Use your time and energy
in a different way.

Martial Arts gives confidence and teaches self-control,
Even bullies can gain the confidence to try a different role.

Check out clever ways to avoid trouble if you can,
Sum up situations, make a self-protection plan.

In this book there's lots of good advice that all children should take,
It's down to you, to do what's right or learn from your mistakes.